Best Animal Stories

Volume I

Aaron A. Vessup

Library of Congress Control Number: 2025913252

ISBN: 979-8-89228-547-6 (Paperback)
ISBN: 979-8-89228-566-7 (Hardcover)
ISBN: 979-8-89228-546-9 (eBook)

Printed in the United States of America

INDEX

THE MOST HAPPY BIRD

Aviator Chicken carries flying notes

By Aaron A. Vessup

Graphics by John Salacan

A small family of birds sing merrily while searching for food on the ground. They march quickly looking among the rocks, leaves, feathers, and among broken twigs from trees. The small birds are chickens. Mother Chickee Lee leads five baby chicks. Chickee Lee-1, Chickee Lee-2, Chickee Lee-3, Chickee Lee-4, and Chickee Lickee Lee, happily search and sing. Overhead the skies are bright blue. This is a sunny day. There are no rain clouds in sight. The chickens are singing:

"We are marching through the land.

Finding food faster than anyone can.

Peep! Peep!

Peep! Peep!

Faster than anyone can.

Hut two... three... four...

Hut two... three... four...

Peep ! Peep!

Peep! Peep!

Faster than anyone can!"X

Mother Chickee Lee's feathers are bright, brown, and shiny. The corners of her mouth point downward making her look sad. But she is not sad. This is the way older chickens look. Her baby Chickees are quite young. The corners of their mouths are straight. They are always smiling because their mouths open wide when hungry. Also, their mouths are wide open when they sing. They are happy hunting for food outside the farm. They are happy hunting for food in the potato fields. And they are happy looking for things to eat in the forest of tall, dark green trees. Sometimes they also sing another song:

"We find great places with smiles on our faces!

Hop a lu a lu!

Hop a lu a lu!"

Chickee Lee-1 is the born first. He is the oldest son. Chickee Lee-2 is a girl, and so was Chickee Lee-3. Chickee Lee-4 is a boy, but, because the last and youngest baby chick was a girl, her name was Chickee-Licky-Lee. She does not walk as fast as the others. She has only two toes on one foot. All the other young chicks and even older chickens have three toes on both of their feet. This makes them walk very fast. But Chickee-Licky-Lee cannot walk fast, so she waddles like a duck. Sometimes she hops like a rabbit. Waddle-waddle, hop-hop. Waddle-waddle, hop-hop.

The group of birds march leaving Paradise Farm and go into the potato fields. A few other baby chicks have now joined the family. These new voices make the group sound louder and happier. Now they walk even faster. Cluck! Cluck! Peep! Peep! Peep! They sing on and on. Their heads poking back and forward with each small quick step.

"We find great places

With smiles on our faces!

Peep! Peep!

Peep! Peep!"

Mother Chicken leads singing group

But soon the sound of voices are far away, and Chickee-Lickee-Lee falls farther behind. She is too tired to hop anymore. And now she no longer hears her brothers and sisters singing. She no longer hears her mother clucking. The sounds of happy singing stops just like magic. All is quiet everywhere. Chickee-Lickee-Lee is lost in the field. Around her she sees big rocks, small brown stones, gray bird feathers, and potatoes.

She is lost indeed. She is tired from hopping like a rabbit. She is tired from waddling like a duck. Little Chickee-Lickee-Lee is all alone. The skies above her change colors from bright blue to solemn gray. Soon she begins to cry.

Suddenly she hears a voice in the quiet air.

"Pisst! Little Birdee! Why are you crying? Whatcha doin' out here in this field alone? Are you lost? Where is your mother?"

The voice had so many questions.

"Where are you?"

The little yellow chicken frantically looks around.

"I'm right over here, sitting under the shady green leaf. See the small brown rock? See me now?"

The bird moves closer trying not to be alarmed. Chickee-Lickee-Lee is curious. Although the sun once had been shining brightly on the pathway, it has disappeared. It is dark in the shade and difficult to see.

Although Chickee-Lickee-Lee is alone and scared, she is not afraid to speak. She is bold and talks.

"Where are you? Are you a rock? What are you?"

At that moment a windy breeze blows slightly. Whrrrrrrr! Whrrrrrr! A large green leaf lifts to reveal a brown object hiding under the leafy plant.

"Come Over here. Come closer. I am not a rock. I am a potato. They call me Mr. Potato Head."

Finally, she finds the potato. The voice looks like a talking stone hiding beneath the large green leaf.

It is like a brown stone that looks strange indeed. There are wrinkles from age on his face with many black spots. Also, long tufts of yellow roots are sticking straight out from the top of his head and chin.

"You are a potato? But you talk. I didn't know any er...ahhh vegetable... uhhh potato could talk.

Feeling surprised at this new discovery, the little chicken smiles a wider smile at the brown potato.

"Well, you're right about that. I am a special potato. If all potatoes could talk then I would not be special. And maybe you would not believe what other potatoes would say if they could talk. But I am a special potato so Great Farmer does not let his workers pick me. Are you lost?"

Again Chickee-Lickey-Lee starts to cry. She tells the potato her troubles.

"It is so difficult to walk in a straight line while singing hunting songs. I am the youngest, smallest, with short legs. Also, I have only two toes instead of three like the others. I think it is stupid to walk so fast looking for food. We get free food mornings and evenings at the Farm during Seed Spreading time."

Mr. Potato understands this problem.

"Hummm. I see."

Then Chickee-lickee-Lee asks some questions.

"Sir, Why do they call you Mr. Potato head? Why don't the farm workers pick you? You do want to be picked don't you?"

And the potato answers.

"Well, I have too many eyes. Anyway, too many eyes and too many root sprouts on the top of my head. Anyway, these eyes have saved me many times. No. I do not want to be picked. Never!"

"Why is that? The Great Farmers could be very happy. I have heard the human workers sing merrily. They clap their hands when returning home with big loads of fresh picked veggies."

"Sorry dear child, you do not understand. Anyway, just like there are all kinds of birds, there are also many kinds of potatoes."

"Really?"

"Yes. Anyway, there are Russettes, Idaho, small yellows, hash browns, pancake, boiled, French fried, twice-baked, chips, and even sweet potatoes."

Mr. Potato Head knows many new things. But what he fears most are mashed potatoes, and a weird place called ***"The Great Kitchen".***

Chickee-Lickee-Lee tries to get the potato to talk more about the "Kitchen", but he just keeps repeating "Anyway..." "Anyway..." and "Sorry...Sorry...I don't really know." Soon Chickee-Lickee-Lee becomes impatient. So, she asked another question.

"Which way is Anyway?"

"Well anyway means F.O.S."

"What does F.O.S. mean?"

Mr. Potato talk to Chickee-Lickee-Lee

Mr. Potato Head sighs.

"My, my, little girl... you have so much to learn. F.O.S. means a **f**igure **o**f **s**peech, okay? If you really need to know more about Kitchens or anything else, just ask your mother. And then, she might ask Pinkie Pig. Your many questions are making my eyes hurt. I cannot close them. I do not know how to blink. Promise me you will ask someone else."

Chickee-Lickee-Lee finally agrees.

"Okay. Okay. I promise. I just want to learn more about the world. And the word "Kitchen" is very new to me. I want to learn as much as I can so my brothers and sisters will stop laughing at me. Just because I am small does not make me stupid. They tease me about my curly feathers. They tease me about my short little legs. And they tease me because I only have two toes on one foot. I must hop when I walk."

"Oh-hhh Chickee-Licky-Lee you are a good girl. I like you because you smile and are not an angry bird. Pay no attention to what others may say. Just beware of Birdmen who come from the Kitchen. Be very careful."

"I know. I know. You are beginning to sound like my mother. Next, you will tell me to keep my feathers clean too. She always says this to me. Today I have learned some new things. There are many types of potatoes. Also, the "Kitchen" is a very special place that many birds visit just like two-legged people. And now you say there are special people called "Birdmen". These are very interesting things!"

"Yes, there are Birdmen to fear, and there are places to fear."

Chickee-Lickee-Lee becomes very excited. She stops crying. She is no longer afraid. When excited she talks faster and faster.

“Wow! My chicken world is small. There are only a few birds. My mother says the Pigeons and Peacocks are the most popular birds in the world. They are very colorful, that’s what she says. My mother says Peacocks have magic feathers. They can even fly. Peacocks are beautiful. My mother closes her eyes and the edges of her mouth look happy when she says, ‘Peacocks are such luuv-a-ly birds!’ When I grow up maybe I will be like a Peacock. This is a good wish I think.”

Mr. Potato Head chuckles kindly.

“What? You mean you only know about Peacocks and Pigeons? Let me tell you this. There are large birds called Swans. These birds have long necks and move with gentle grace in the water. Also, there is another bird called a Goose. Geese have large strong wings and can fly around the world. They see and know many things! Do you know there is a bird called the Wise Owl? His head can turn around like a spinning top. Have you not seen any Waterfowl?”

Now, Chickee-Lickee-Lee has more questions to ask.

“What’s a Waterfowl? I have not been near the river because I have just started to march free-ranging a few days ago.”

“Oh, I see. So you do not know about quacking ducks, graceful swans, and powerful strong honking geese.”

“No. Do these big birds fly?”

“Yes, they have wings much different than yours, and they can fly many miles away. They see many things you cannot see on the ground.”

So, is this why my mum is always telling me to take care of myself, keep my wings clean, exercise, and be careful? I know how to avoid hissing purple-eyed Snakes that spit, and the large-toothed Crocodiles. But why must I plump and fluff my feathers so much? Mother makes me clean every hour."

"You must listen to your mother more. Do you know any happy songs?"

"Well...uh..."

"Can you sing the happy song about how to stop being worried?"

"No..."

"Well, I can teach it to you a special song."

But before Mr. Potato Head can begin, suddenly their conversation is interrupted by a new voice. It was very loud.

"WHERE ARE YOU? CHICKEE-LICKEE-LEE...WHERE ARE YOU-U-U-U?!"

Mr. Potato urges the young chicken to answer the call.

"Oops. That must be your mom. She is searching for you."

"Yep. Probably. She gets a little worried all the time when I do not stay in line behind my older brothers and sisters. She says the fresh smell of green pine trees is refreshing. But I get tired of looking at feathers in front of me when I am following someone. I have never seen pine trees up close. But I want to see the world."

But, Mr. Potato insists that she must leave.

“Listen to your mom and keep your eyes wide open. The world is a very strange place. It has many challenges. Remember that some birds are even special. Maybe you are special too. Only time will tell. Goodbye my little friend. Good luck!”

Mr. Potato smiles and Chickee Lickee Lee smiles. Then she moves toward the middle of the path so that her mother easily finds her. Several other small chickees are following close behind the Mother chicken. On the path are many small, gray and white pigeon feathers. But she does not have time to pick up anything. She is happy to see her family again. Also, she was happy because now she has a new friend. A Potato.

“Mommie! I was talking to Mr. Potato Head.”

But Momma Chicken is just relieved to see her lost youngster.

“Oh! There you are. Cluck. Cluck. Cluck. Please follow us and stop that nonsense. There is no one here but us. Cluck. Cluck. Cluck. We have no time to play with brown rocks. There is no such thing as a brown rock that talks. Come along children! Come now! Cluck. Cluck. Cluck. Let’s go! Soon it will be dark. We have been looking everywhere for you. Hurry up! It’s almost dinner seed spreading time. Come along now! Follow me children! Cluck. Cluck. Cluck.”

And without another word Momma Chickee Lee marches away. THe large group of yellow chicks closely follow. The wind is not blowing so the potato is hiding again beneath a large green leaf. Momma Chickee Lee cannot see the old potato. No one is singing now. Perhaps they were all much too tired. And so, Chickee-Lickee-Lee waves goodbye to her potato friend. Darkness is rapidly falling. But she hears Mr. Potato’s fading voice call out.

“Be careful my little friend, keep your eyes sharp on the lookout. There are dangerous things flying in the air. But you will find a great place to keep that smile on your face! Goodbye!”

At last the marching chickens reach the Paradise Farm just in time for dinner. The little chickees are all so tired, almost too tired to eat.

Later that evening after the Seed Spread Feast, the birds are resting. Now the little chickens are comfortable in the warm woody smells of straw and sweet hay. Little Chickee-Lickee-Lee tells her two brothers and two sisters some things Mr. Potato Head has told her. But they did not believe her.

"Mom, Chickee-Lickee-Lee says there are birds that fly with strong, long feathers, and birds like giraffes with long necks, birds that swim gracefully in water."

"Mom, Can we make honking sounds when we grow up? I want to grow strong wings with smart feather that can fly high up in the trees."

"Not me! I just want a long neck and make smooth circles in the water pond." This was Chickee Lee-2.

Then Chickee Lee-3 says something that startles Chickee-Lickee-Lee.

"Today, when you were lost, we saw a bird floating above us with colorful feathers. Mother said this a Parrot."

"We saw a Parrot."

"We saw a Parrot."

"We saw a Parrot."

They repeat themselves like Mockingbirds. Then Chickee Lee-4 says something else that is also strange and new.

"We also saw a Rabbit hopping along almost like your style of walking, but it was faster. He had feathers that were thick and bushy like yours!"

But Chickee-Lickee-Lee does not agree.

"Those were not feathers, the rabbit wears fur clothes!"

There was a bit of disagreement among the other Chickee Lee kids. But then Chickee Lee-1 speaks louder with spite in his voice to his smaller little sister.

"Chickie-Lickee-Lee, you look like a yellow rabbit. You walk like a slow rabbit and waddle like a duck. I bet your wings will never grow to let you fly. You cannot even fight without strong wings!"

Mother Chickee Lee interrupts to tell the children they should not think about becoming fighters.

"Your late father was very popular before you were born. He was a fighter I am sad to say. He had very strong feathers and fast, sharp feet. The Birdmen took him away and made him fight other birds. Your father was known as 'Great Feather Claw'. They say Birdmen became very wealthy because your father won many fights against other birds. But now your father has disappeared. No one knows where he is, or if he is even alive. Who knows if any of this was really true. I miss your father very much."

Chickee Lee-1 speaks out.

"I want to be like my father. I want to fight and fly!"

Other voices chime in expressing similar dreams.

Special exercise area for training fighters

By now other young chickens began to make “Peep, Peep”, noises, but their voices are drowned out by the general ruckus now in the Henhouse.

There are clucking sounds and wings beating against the air. All of the birds are happy. But they are still too young to go to school.

The young birds have many questions. The mother Chickee Lee tries to answer each of her little Chickees. They all are very excited. Also, other ears in the Hen House are listening. Soon the entire group in the Hen House becomes very noisy. Now many older adult chickens flap their wings to exercise and shout. "Cluck! Cluck! Cluck! Cluck!" Clucking and more clucking. These sounds older chickens naturally make. The noises they make cause the Farmer to send his workers to look inside the Hen House. Perhaps the birds are upset because a poisonous snake is nearby, or four-legged sharp toothed fox is staring at them. Some people believe that just because birds are noisy they are unhappy. This is not always true.

But all of this talk makes Chickee-Lickee-Lee keep silent. She is very tired.

In her mind, she wonders about many things. She has heard the adult talk about strange things. Grown chickens always worry about the length of their legs, or whether their feathers would be strong enough to fly up to the treetops. They compare themselves to the Wise Owl. He has thick feathers. And He has been known to say that perhaps some birds should learn to fly. It is safer to live high in the trees. But Chickee-Lickee-Lee has never seen Wise Owl. She is too small and she cannot get up stair steps much less into trees. But sometimes she hears the voices of Wise Owl or the Master Rooster talking and making speeches. They say things like:

"You were born to be only one of three things: You could be a fighter, a flyer, or a fryer. This simply means some birds can fight with their beaks and claws sharpened into deadly weapons. This life offers a chance to become famous. All famous birds get special treatment like a king or queen. If not this, some chickens were special enough to fly away when their feather are right, wings strong, and the weather cooperates. But, if these two things did not happen, a chicken's fate will be a trip to a place called *"The Great Kitchen".* In that place a chicken becomes food for the two-legged farm people to eat. A good chicken is always fat and happy.

Some adult chickens like to repeat the pledge, “Fight, Fly, or Fry!”

But when Wise Owl hoots and talks, his head spins at certain times around in a complete circle. This frightens most of the chickens, so they did not trust all of his words. His spinning head and wide white eyes looked very strange. Someone said Wise Owl could even ride buses with humans. Another voice claimed Wise Owl was seen driving a human bus. This strange information causes a ruckus again in the Hen house, and now the birds squawk and cluck louder and longer. Only some of these voices are angry birds. However, most of the birds become very excited hearing these things.

Later that night Chickee Lickee-1, the older brother, again starts to argue. The topic never seems to change. Many other young chicks also join in. You can hear different voices complaining against Chickee-Lickee-Lee:

“I bet you think you are smarter than we are. Because you talked to a brown stone called Mr. Potato Head, you think that you know a lot.”

“We still say all pigeons are black, just like crows. And they all are the same size.”

“Even the Magpie bird is black and eats the same things we eat.”

“Chickens never fly. We are supposed to become proud owners of strong drumsticks. Our thighs are highly prized.”

“But you, Chickee-Lickee-Lee, have short legs and small fluffy wings. Clearly, you will never be strong enough to fly high up into the treetops. Only special birds can do this. Maybe you are really a duck. Perhaps you will swim away in water.”

There is no agreement on these topics even though the chickens are whispering. However, their voices become louder and louder. Soon other ears can hear their voices. More feathered chicks chime in talking and debating. They keep making "peep-peeping" sounds as if they are hungry. And so, the adult hens and Rudy Rooster must warn them to quiet down.

"Cluck. Cluck. Shssh! Shssh! Calm down. Calm down. Be quiet. Cluck. Cluck."

"If you keep peeping you will become hoarse and your throat will hurt. You will never be able to croon, Cocka-doodle do-oo-o, in the morning like Rudy Rooster. Your throats need rest to grow strong. Do you want to become hoarse?"

Other chickens agree, but some did not. One chicken now makes a clear point.

"No chicken has ever grown four legs to run like a horse! This is impossible!"

So, on and on they argue about differences between feeling painfully hoarse in the throat, and actually becoming a horse.

But then someone says that if talking too loud does not turn you into a horse, in the end your voice will make croaking sounds like a frog: Rivert! Rivert! Rivert!

The birds laugh and laugh. Soon the entire chicken coop vibrates with mocking frog sounds loud and long. It is noisy in the Hen house.

"Rivert! Verbert!! Ribart!! Rivat! Rivat! Rivat! Rivert, rivert, rivert!"

But as the birds became tired some birds disagree again. Their faces look stern and grim.

Pinkie Pig says "frogs make Rivert! Rivert! noises because they are thirsty or hungry for insects."

Other birds say,

"Ugh! That's so disgusting. Frogs eating insects is strange. This does not sound like a tasty dish at all!"

A soft voice says, “Ohh... but this must be true.”

But suddenly they hear a loud voice above their heads outside of the Hen House.

“Hoot! Hoot! Who-o-o? Hoot! Hoot! Who-o-o? Is there a problem inside the coop? Hoot! Who-o-o? Who has a problem?”

This is Wise Owl. They know his voice. He sounds like deep warbling words in a thick ball of cotton. Although inside the Hen house birds cannot see Wise Owl, other birds say he is wise, because he looks like a thick, wide book. His eyes are wide just like small dinner plates. And some say Wise Owl is a flying Dictionary because he knows many words. Wise Owl had seen many things in the world outside the Great Farm. So, he speaks often to them. The Owl says,

“Listen, I will tell you the truth in this matter. It only makes sense that frogs make croaking noises. However, saying ‘Rivert’ is not their speech. The ‘Rivert’ sounds come from frogs who are coughing. This is unfortunate.”

Then a curious voice asks an important question.

“Really? Then why do frogs cough only at night?”

The Owl quickly answers.

“The frogs cough in the night because they smoke cigarettes all day. This smoking makes their throats dry and itchy. They cannot stop coughing a lot. So let this be a warning to you: stay away from smoking cigarettes. Do Not Smoke. If you want your legs to grow long, and your wings to become strong, do not smoke anything in your mouths.”

However, some birds protest. Some Chickens do not always trust the wide bird with a spinning head. They have heard curious rumors about his social activities. But, this time, most of the chickens agree that

Wise Owl's wisdom is great. They have never seen frogs, but only heard their sounds at night. They do not even know the color of a frog's eyes. The Owl must be wise. He had seen much in the world beyond Paradise Farm. Soon the birds began a group chant that lasts far into the night. Finally, they all fall asleep.

Suddenly, A single voice cries out a warning while dreaming.

"Don't Smoke! Don't Smoke! Don't Smoke! Or you will croak! Don't smoke! Don't Smoke! Don't Smoke or you will croak!"

And then, another voice murmurs, "Fight, fly, or fry. Fight, fly, or fry..... Fry, fry, fry!" These must be Parrots who simply cannot stop talking.

And now, most chickens are already dreaming about the delicious aromas from corn seeds that smell like fresh creamy milk. While sleeping perhaps chickens think they are chewing popcorn. These dreamers sleep with mouths wide open.

Chickee-Lee Imagines future goals

But little Chickee-Lickee-Lee does not hear words or noises in the dark night. She is already asleep. She dreams about gray and white Pigeon feathers scattered on the ground. Maybe she should study them. Maybe she should even search for Peacock feathers. They must really be beautiful. Her head is resting on a soft cloud of feathers, and feels comfortable. She thinks perhaps she can learn to fly before anyone in her family. Maybe she is already flying. Chickee-Lickee-Lee smiles to herself. Deeper and deeper she sleeps feeling happier and happier.

Tomorrow she must remember to ask her mother to teach her the happy song. Then she will never worry or be afraid anymore. Also, perhaps the Peacock must really be a luu-va-lee bird. Maybe tomorrow she can find a magical Peacock feather. Many hours pass before this sleeping little chicken hears Rudy Rooster's call to wake all the sleepers. This will be the time for another Happy Day of exciting adventures.

[photo image by Aaron A. Vessup]

////////// THE END /////////

HONEY BEAR AND THE BEES

Honey Bear Practicing Magic

By Aaron A. Vessup

Graphics by Sonny Gergen

The Bear is lazy. He does not like to work.

"When I Say Magic. I See the Magic."

Mr. Bear repeats this phrase as he leans against a tall tree in the shade.

"When I Say magic. I See the Magic."

Today Mr. Bear is very hungry.

As he leans against the tall tree, his sharp claws are safely folded away. His large shoulders

Push and scrape the thick bark on the tree trunk. Hunger cramps make his stomach feel pain.

"When I Say Magic. I see the Magic!"

With his eyes shut he repeats this phrase again and again. He is indeed hungry. His stomach pain does not go away. The bear has been repeating these words for a long while. Winter indeed is coming soon. He must have food in his stomach. A long sleep during hibernation is essential. So now his voice wails louder. He is almost groaning.

"WHEN I SAY MAGIC. I SEE THE MAGIC!"

However, because he listens to many stories about Harry Potter, in his mind he believes he can also do magic. He thinks he can make magic work to get food and drink. Then he can be called a Magician.

If only he can say the correct words, perhaps magic can happen for him. He is certain this is the way to get something without working.

Just at that moment a colorful red and yellow parrot flying overhead hears the bear talking to himself.

This is strange indeed. The bird is surprised because he also speaks words as well.

“Wha…wha….what did you say?” The bird asked. “When you what?”

Mr. Bear opens his eyes. Looking up he repeats his words again.

“I say magic. I see magic.”

“What is this? Why are you saying this? Are you trying to make a spectacle of yourself?”

“No, I am not trying to make spectacles. I am very hungry” said the bear. “I want to make food appear so I can eat.”

Parrot and Honey bear Disagree about Magic

"Well, that's easy. To eat, you must do something, not just talk. You are a silly bear. You are making a spectacle. Goodbye."

And the colorful parrot flew away above the trees. The Bear is surprised that the bird has even spoken to him. Normally flying things in the air do not speak to four-footed creatures on the ground.

For several days the bear does nothing. He returns to his favorite places to rest and relax his mind. Some days he sleeps longer in his bed at home. On other days he floats on a raft in the river.

When he opens his eyes just looking up at the sky, seeing fluffy white clouds make him feel good. The bear's stomach begins to rumble again. Indeed, he is hungry and just like the parrot had said, perhaps he should do something to make magic work. Perhaps just saying a few words is not enough.

Honey Bear habit is laziness never working

****

Can you guess what happens next?

********?@@? ********

Animals observe strange Bear behaviors

The bear begins to hug a tall tree. He wraps his two long hairy arms around the tree trunk. He squeezes the tree trunk. As he does this, his large belly scrapes the tree trunk.

When doing so, a large tree branch pokes the house of a Bee family. The beehive is a honeycomb. This house is usually filled with gallons of thick, golden, creamy sweet honey. However, when the tree branch pokes the honeycomb, rich liquid starts to drip down. Some of the honey drops on the bear's nose making a pitter-patter sounds.

"Plip. Plop. Plip- Plop. Plip. Plip. Plop-Plop."

The bear feels something on his nose. Immediately his long pink tongue lashes out. He licks the sweet honey. Now, he opens his mouth open wider. Then he squeezes the tree trunk harder with his strong arms. More sweet honey pours into his mouth.

"Hmmm! Hummm! Hummm!!" His tongue is very busy. The honey comes faster and faster.

Plip-plip-plip. Plop-plop-plop! Now more honey hits the bear's nose. He rubs his belly against the tree and squeezes harder. The bear's mouth opens wider than ever.

Sweet honey streams down into his throat like a fountain of sweet, delicious water.

"Oh my god!" said the bear.

"Oh my god. oh my god, oh my god! I have done magic! I say magic, I see magic. I am a Magician just like Harry Potter! Oh, my goodness!"

Then the bear opens his eyes. He could not see the Bee's honey house. It is too far up high in the trees. It is covered with many green tree leaves. The Bear does not know where the honey comes from. To him this all seems like true magic.

That night while at home, Mr. Bear only thinks and dreams about saying magic words for food to eat. The bear is surprised at his good fortune. He must try magic to get something to chew on. Tasting meat is now on his mind.

Early the next morning the bear leaves his cave to try magic words for food. As he slowly ambles close to a small pond, Freddy Frog hops from the grass into the water. The bear does not see the frog, because he is trying to remember the magic words used yesterday.

He keeps mumbling, "Say Magnetic... See Mystic. Say...Mystic, see Magnetic."

Sadly, the bear had forgotten the proper words.

And at this moment, Freddy Frog is out for an afternoon adventure. He is always ready for action. His light green legs with dark spots flash in the sunlight. He hops and springs from one point to the next. He moves very fast. Quickly he hops again from the water and lands on a lily pad floating in the pond. His red tongue flickers quickly out of his mouth to catch a fly. Seconds later even a mosquito is also unlucky. Freddy Frog hops, stops, flicks out his red tongue. He eats and swallows. But then he hears a voice speaking. So, he stops chewing to listen. The voice is Mr. Bear.

"Mr. Bear, is that you? Why are you making such a ruckuss? You should be home taking a nap. Are you trying to make a spectacle of yourself? Why are you so noisy?"

"Ahhh ha!" Said the bear. "It is no time to sleep. I can do magic. I am a Magician."

"What? Have you gone crazy? Bears cannot do magic."

"Sorry Freddy. Sorry. You are so small and too far away. At your distance you could never see my magic. You must be closer. It is really true. I say magic, and I see magic."

"Rubbish! I don't believe you." Said Freddy Frog.

"Well, come closer and you will believe me. Come on. Hop off that lily pad and land on the ground."

"Okay, said Freddy Frog."

And he hopped from the water into the grass near the bear's feet.

"Good. That's good." Said the bear.

"Now I will close my eyes. You must hop high in the air as I say the magic words."

The bear closes only one eye. He watches and waits for the frog to hop. Then he says the words that had worked before.

"I say magic, I see the magic."

And just as Freddy Frog jumps the bear quickly snatches him from the air. He plops the frog into his mouth and gobbles it up. Head, legs, and all slide inside the bear's huge throat. As he disappears the frog makes croaking sounds.

"Rrrribbit...Rrrribbit....Rrrribbit! Glunk! Glunk!!"

"Ahhh...that was tasty" said the bear. He licks his lips over his sharp teeth. Now his stomach is bigger and he feels satisfied. Today he is no longer hungry. Then he thinks, yesterday, I had honey from magic. Today I have frog legs from magic. Perhaps tomorrow, from magic, I shall eat fish.

I am not making spectacles. I shall find some glasses to wear like Harry Potter. Harry Potter is a fine magician. He wears spectacles over his eyes. If I wear spectacles I will be just like Harry Potter. A magic man.

So guess what happened next?

*******?@@?*******

That night Mr. Bear went home to his cave. Under the bed, he searched. In every corner of the cave he searched. He also looked in a large collection of things tourists had lost. There is a stack of forgotten items campers had left behind. Old books, cans of sardines, and cookies. Even small boxes he cannot open.

He also has a collection of fishing equipment, leather wallets, and plastic purses. Then smaller items are discovered: a toothbrush, a plastic cup, two wooden pencils, and other odds and ends. After a long time passes the Bear finds a pair of Sunglasses.

Mr. Bear finds sunglasses to wear

"Ahhh. This will do nicely," he said, as he places them over his eyes. "I will show those fools that I am a real magician like Harry Potter. Wearing these spectacles tomorrow will certainly convince them that I am right."

The next day, Mr. Bear ambles slowly to the riverbank where fish are jumping and flying upstream. The bear sees black Rainbow Trout and long silvery Salmon.

Rudy Rabbit hops by and stops to watch. His white fur glows brightly in the shadows. His long floppy ears twitch nervously. In one hand the rabbit holds a green cucumber. In the other hand is a bright orange carrot. He nibbles first on the carrot, then on the cucumber. His pink nose twitches and ears wiggle. His large white teeth chomp down on these vegetables. Each bite makes an echo in his head.

"Nibble! Nibble! Chomp! Chomp!"

But the water is so noisy that only the rabbit hears these sounds in his head. The Rabbit chews and nibbles.

"Chomp! Chomp! Chomp!"

Mr. Bear was wading into the moving water, but now he sits on a rock. Finally, Rudy Rabbit stops eating and speaks.

"Good morning Mr. Bear. Why are you wearing glasses? Indeed, you are making a spectacle of yourself sitting on a rock wearing glasses?"

"No, I am not making any spectacles. I am a Magician just like Harry Potter. And I make magic happen, not spectacles." The bear angrily replied.

"Humpf!" Said Rudy Rabbit. "I don't believe you. Show me."

Mr. Bear touches a tree as honey drips into his mouth

“Okay. Watch and learn.” Said Mr. Bear.

Then the rabbit quietly watches. He hears the Bear say these words.

“I want some salmon fish to eat. I say magic, I see magic. I say magic, I see magic. I say magic, I see magic.”

Mr. Bear has both of his eyes open. And suddenly a large fish jumps out of the water. It is flying in the air near Mr. Bear. And quicker than a rat-trap can snap, the bear grabs the fish with his mouth right out of the air.

Then he climbed down from the rock and climbs out of the river. He sits down and enjoys his meal.

But the rabbit was not fooled. He is not convinced that this has been magic. This was nothing like the famous Harry Potter. And the rabbit protests.

"No-no-no- no- no! That was not magic. Any bear can do that. I have seen other bears catch Salmon without saying any words at all! You are not a Magician. You are not like Harry Potter!"

"Say what you will," said the bear, "I know these words work, and my magic is real! Perhaps you are jealous of my skills."

"I am not!"

"Yes, you are!"

"I am not!"

"You are!"

"Not!"

****

And guess what happened next?

*********?@@?********

A Wise Owl sat high in the tall tree listening. The two arguing creatures, bear and rabbit were now Shouting.

After a while he decides to help settle the conflict about Magic or No magic.

"Listen, gentlemen. Stop and Listen! Please! I will tell you how to prove whether our friend who wears sunglasses is a magic man like Harry Potter. Would you like to know?"

The bear and rabbit stop arguing and listen to the Wise Owl's advice.

"Tomorrow, Let's go to the first tree where Mr. Bear claims he worked magic. Let us see if he can bring honey again when he says those magic words. Okay?"

So, the next day they all meet at the tree where Mr. Bear claims his magic began. This had been his tree of good fortune. Again today, Mr. Bear is hungry.

Animals try to change the Bear's mind

Many creatures around have heard the news about this meeting. Some of the birds and animals decide to protest and persuade Honey Bear to change his mind. They are not happy. In their minds this bear is setting a bad example for others in the community. Squirrels, sparrows, and black crows perch themselves on tree limbs to watch every day. And then one day they see Honey Bear actually lean against a tree. He wraps his arms around the tree trunk and mumbles words. He repeats the same words again and again.

The rabbit is very amused. He starts laughing.

"Oh-oh! I think Mr. Bear is a looney. Ha! Ha! Ha! He looks like a fat Santa Claus. So stupid! Look how his large belly is rubbing the bark off the tree trunk. His belly only needs a red coat and wide black belt. Then he would be Santa's fat Helper. Ha! Ha! Ha!'

And all the silent onlookers also began to laugh. The sparrows and crows. Joined in. Some animals start chanting loudly:

"Fat! Fat! Caw! Caw! Fat! Fat! Santa Claus!"

"Fat! Fat! Caw! Caw! Fat! Fat! Santa Claus!"

But the Bear closes his eyes and squeezes the tree trunk tighter and harder with his arms.

His eyes remain shut as he mumbles,

"I say magic, I see magic. I say magic, I see magic. I say magic, I see magic."

And just like in the beginning a sharp branch poked another hole in the house of bees. And just as before honey began to drip, drip, drip. And then suddenly honey pour down from the honeycomb.

But this time something else happened. It is true that the bees are usually very busy. However, the Queen Bee had noticed a few days ago that honey had mysteriously disappeared from their home. Now all the Bees are concerned. Therefore, Queen Bee has posted four Bees, called "Drones" to act as guards. They are special Bees on alert watching for any unusual event. They cannot allow their home to be destroyed.

"Plop-plop. Plip-plip. Plop-plop. Pli-i-i-ip!"

Downstream the honey onto the bear's nose and into his mouth. His long pink tongue licks faster and faster to keep up with the stream of sweet honey.

Down from the tree also came the four Drone bees. They follow the stream of honey and hovered around the large nose of Mr. Bear.

And guess what happened?

*******?@@?*******

The angry Bees sting the Bear

///// THE END /////

HAPPY BIRDS GO TO SCHOOL

classroom scene

by Aaron A. Vessup

Graphics by Sonny Gergen

[[A Wise Owl moonlights at night Watching. However, during the day he is Head Teacher at the Bird Brain School. It is here where certain bird types learn rules for safer living.]]

Admission Day WELCOME

In the Bird Brain School, Wise Owl is very busy observing, learning, and instructing. When outside the building he gathers information at night. Inside the classrooms during the day he is teaching. Wise Owl had many different students. These students are birds of many sizes. Many are small, but a few are large. And these birds are of many different colors like a rainbow.

Some residents at Paradise Farm think Wise Owl is a fat bird. Others believe that Wise Owl's body is big and wide because he actually eats words for food. Perhaps this means he likes eating hot alphabet soup. Also, his large eyes see many things. However, something is strange about his big eyes. Each eye is the size of small dinner plates, and one eye is bright yellow, and the other eye was blue.

Some kind words describe him as being a short, stout bird, with strong sturdy wings for flying at night. He is also very brave. This bird does not fear animals, and does not fear humans. Some unkind words about Wise Owl are that his fat, large belly, is like a heavy pot. This keeps him from flying far from the Paradise Farm. The unkind people believe the Owl is blind and lazy. But good parents believe the Owl is the wisest bird knowing how to avoid danger. This bird lives more years than most other birds.

Yet, despite these rumors, Wise Owl sees many things and knows many secrets. Some things he does not tell anyone. But all the birds listen to him, because he is very kind and wise. Therefore, all older birds send their young birds to school. Bird Brain School is famous for producing outstanding students. These birds survive in the world no matter where they fly to live.

Dangers to Avoid

Wise Owl has a very strange voice. He will say,

“Hoot! Hoot! Whooooo... Hoot Hoot! Whooooo....”

No other bird could say this. They did not know how to copy his hoots.

When Wise Owl speaks all birds become silent. No one laughs. No one says “Peep! Peep! Peep!”, or even cry. No one sings happily.

“Hoot! Hoot! Whoooo... Hoot! Hoot! Whoooo...”

The students in the classroom are only birds. But sadly, some birds are not welcome into this special schoolhouse. Young Buzzards and Vultures are okay, but the older ones were not welcome. Young Bald Eagles and Sky Hawks were welcome, but the older ones were not. Any bird beyond 3 years is not admitted into this school. Except for Rudy Rooster who works there as the school guardian.

This red-headed older chicken had sharp steel tips for his toes and a sharp golden claw on each leg. Peacocks of any size or age are also not admitted because they were too pretty. These birds take up too much room with their long, beautiful feathers. Other birds might become jealous if Peacocks were to become the Teacher’s favorite bird. They would be unhappy. Other birds would tease them shouting words like:

“Teacher’s pet!”

“Teacher’s Pet!”

This cannot be allowed to happen.

And one more thing. Hummingbirds, sadly cannot be admitted into Bird Brain School. These tiny birds make too much noise with their humming wing sounds. Also, Hummingbirds cannot stop moving or be quiet for ten seconds.

But, all of the birds at this school enjoy the Wise Owl Teacher. They love him because he tells exciting stories filled with happy adventures. The Owl teaches young birds many new things about the world outside Paradise Farm.

He talks about seeing fish with no legs, animals with four legs, and Birdmen who stand very tall on two legs.

Some of the students are very young almost like babies. Perhaps the youngest boy and girl birds are only 4 weeks old. Some little birds cry when they do not see their mothers or fathers nearby. Some birds are older. Some birds are brave, some birds are afraid of things like the sound of the wind blowing. Some birds cannot even say “Peep! Peep! Peep!”

Yet, there were other very young birds in class. Some are 5, 6, and 7 months old. Old Rudy Rooster watches to keep order. This is his second job. However, each morning his first job is to wake everyone up SHOUTING,

“Cock-a-doodle-doo! Cock-a-doodle-doo!!!”

In school, the students learn to say, “Good Morning Teacher Owl!”

“Good Afternoon Teacher Owl!” and

“Good Night Teacher Owl!”

Today, is the first day in school. It is cold and chilly outside. But this is a sunny September day. And so, after everyone says, “Good morning!” The birds exercise shaking their cold bodies, shivering, and smoothing down the fluffy feathers on their wings.

After these exercises, the first lesson begins. With so many birds in class each day, the room is hot and stuffy. The musty smells of wet bird feathers is everywhere. Teacher Owl’s voice sounds like worbly cotton balls inside a deep well of water. The teacher asks a question.

“Class... Hoot! Hoot! Whooo....knows...... what the name of today is?”

"Today is Monday", tweets the small brown bird. This was Brown Sparrow.

"No, no, no!" Coos the older Pigeon, "Today is Tuesday...Coo! Coo!"

"Quack! Quack!" The Quacker Duck disagrees,

"There is no day called Two-Days! No such thing. There are only Mondays and Fridays! I know this because people with two legs only fry food in *The Great Kitchen* on the last day."

Another duck agrees and says,

"Let us all say Quack! Quack!"

"Quack! Quack! For Mondays!"

"Quack! Quack! For Fridays!"

"Caw! Caw! Not so fast", said the Black Crow,

"Food fries first every day at fast food places. Today is the only day for those who are not weak people!

The classroom is noisy. Many students sit with grim faces. Their lips stretch tight like thin lines of string. Teacher Owl silently watches. His big eyes are wide. He waits. His eyes do not blink. His head begins to spin around in a slow circle. He thinks about flying in the night while everyone sleeps.

The students do not know that Teacher Owl has many secrets. He is called Big Eyes Owl by the older birds and chickens who did not go to school. He is Teacher at school, but Mister Big Eyes Owl at night. He sees everything. So, he has two names. At night he can "Hoot" as many times as he likes. But as Teacher in the classroom he could only say "Hoot! Hoot!" two times before each important lesson. And so, suddenly the Teacher Owl has an idea.

“Hoot! Hoot! Classss. Attention! Classss.”

“Hoot! Hoot! Whooooo!”

The room now becomes quiet.

“Today we will talk about the importance of smiling. Yes, we need to really know how and when to smile.”

Some of the students are shocked. They do not move any feathers. They do not even shiver. But not, Polly Blue Parrot with a hook nose. His nose and beak are shaped like an upside-down question mark. He is not shocked to sit still.

“Wha! Wha!! What is Smelling about? Why do we need to learn about Smelling? We must talk about nuts and corn, things I like to eat!”

And then Turkey Lurky with his bushy feather interrupts.

“Gobble! Gobble!” “Gobble! Gobble! Gobble!”

Other birds want him to be quiet, because he only Says,

‘Gobble! Gobble!’ and nothing else.

The SMELL vs. SMILE Lesson

"Shhhh! Please be quiet! Shhhh!"

Old Rudy Rooster will not have any of this noise and disagreement. His job is to keep order in the class of learning. He must say Cock-a-doodle-doo when he wants order and quiet.

"We are not going to learn about Smelling. We are going to learn about Smiling. There is a big difference."

"Cock-a-doodle-doooo!"

Teacher Owl agreed.

"Very good Rudy Rooster. You are correct. These two words are quite different. Now, all of you please look at the corners of your own mouth. And now look at your nose. What do you see? Are all of your mouths shaped the same? Do your noses smell the same aromas.

"No! No!" One student answers.

"I smell Earl!"

Hearing this, everyone laughed. And then someone else shouts,

"No! You smell like oil, not Earl!"

Many birds keep laughing softly. They are so amused. Then Brown Sparrow makes a suggestion.

"It's too stuffy inside the school room, let's go outside!"

This time everyone ignores the Brown bird. These birds want to learn more new things.

Teacher Owl asks questions again.

"Do all of your mouths appear the same? Does your nose only notice stinky things.

Many students quickly reply:

"No! No! Some things smell good!"

"I smell sweet hay!"

"I smell honeycombs!"

All of the birds tweet and chirp.

“We look differently, and things smell nice and others not so nice. This all depends on what we each like. We are different.”

“This is Correct”, said Teacher Owl.

“Your mouth can be happy when you open it to eat. Your nose is above your mouth and you can smell your food with your nose. You do not eat with your nose. When your mouth is smiling you will feel happy and not afraid. This is your happy life. Eating. Smiling and not frying in *The Great*-two-legged *Kitchen*.”

And so, Teacher Owl talks on and on.... But suddenly the mobile phone in his pocket started to ring.

Bzzz! Bzzz!

Bzzz! Bzzz!

Before the teacher could answer his phone Brown Sparrow exclaimed,

“Oh! It must be Lunch-Time! Time to eat! Time to Eat! We must go... time to...”

The Black Crows agreed, and with a few loud “Caw! Caws!” they fly outside.

And suddenly more bird wings are flapping and waving. Before Teacher Owl says another word more birds rise into the air. Some birds flew out a window. Others out the door.

The birds scatter in many directions before Rudy Rooster could say “Cock-a-doodle doo!” Their wings fluttered noisily, and Teacher Owl’s head begins to spin faster and faster. However, all of the students do not disappear. Some were simply just too slow.

For instance, Turkey Lurky was fat, with thick bushy hind feathers, and stumpy legs. He squawks and squawks hoping the other birds would wait.

"Gobble! Gobble!"

"Gobble! Gobble! Wait for me!"

But it is too late. The other birds are gone. They did not know what "Gobble! Gobble!" means. Plus, the student birds are not sure if the fat Turkey really wanted to eat them for lunch. Perhaps "Gobble! Gobble!" Means Turkey Lurky is hungry.

Birds leaving class early without permission

Soon after lunch the student birds slowly return. Their bellies are filled with food. They are very happy and chat noisily. They are ready to learn new things again. Teacher Owl's head is no longer spinning.

"Hoot! Hoot! Now class! Attention! Let's continue our studies. Here are pieces of paper I will give to each of you. Please draw a picture of your favorite food you eat on this paper. Make a picture for the class to see what you like. You will have five minutes to do your best work. This should be a pleasing time for you."

Students think about favorite food drawing Project

But Turkey Lurky is confused. He does not know what the word "pleasing" means. In fact, he thinks the Teacher Owl said to draw a picture of a Pheasant bird. He knows about Pheasant birds because sometimes Birdmen with two legs say he is small like a Pheasant. And so, Turkey Lurky draws a picture of a Pheasant bird.

Soon it is time for the students to share their work. Teacher Owl claps his wings in front of his wide body and hoots.

"Hoot! Hoot! Attention Classss! Time to share. Let us all see your Art work."

First, to share was Chickee-Lickee-Lee... She proudly shows the class an orange carrot and yellow kernel of corn. The student birds make "Ooh!" and "Ahh!" sounds!

Someone asked, "You like to eat carrots? I thought only rabbits could eat carrots."

"Yes, I like creamy corn seeds and also sweet tiny carrots."

"Ohhh, you are so brave!"

Another voice says, "That looks so Nice!"

And the birds all smile, so Chickee-Lickee-Lee is very happy.

Food Favorites, Carrot and Corn

The second bird to share is Brown Sparrow. His picture is images of tiny ants and sunflower seeds..... Again the student birds "ooh!" and "ahh!" They all smile. Large Polly Red Parrot, and also the smaller Polly Blue Parrot clap their wings with joy while repeating,

"Fabulous! Fabulous!"

These words came from the colorful Parrots, Polly Red Parrot and Polly Blue Parrot. Both are smart birds. They can say many English words just like two-legged people. Some words are nice, and some words not so nice for tender ears to hear.

So, Brown Sparrow is happy.

Next, the third bird to share is Black Crow. He has drawn a picture of long, thin, brown and red shiny worms. And again all the student birds say "Oooh!" and "Awe!" They all smile. Black Crow's red eyes gleam with happiness. Teacher Owl even clapped his wing with encouragement. The Wise Owl's eyes did not even blink.

At last, Turkey Lurkey shows his picture surprise... the Pheasant bird. Everyone gasped loudly in shock. They did not say "ooh" and "awe". Not one bird said one peep. Each student looks at the baby turkey with fear in their eyes. Their mouths are all closed tight, looking sad and grim.

At first, they have no words to say. Then a brave...voice asks...

"Do birds eat other birds?"

And so, Teacher Owl talks about rules and proper things birds should eat. Birds do not need to beg for food. Squirrels beg. Monkeys beg. But, smart birds hunt and work for their own food.

He said, all birds should not eat fish. Only a bird who knows how to fish should eat the creatures that swim in the water. Some birds have strong wings and can fly very high to suddenly dive into the water and catch fish. This bird is called the King Fisher. This unusual bird is not afraid to go deep under the water.

Again the students says "Ohhhh!" and "Ahhhh!" They are surprised to hear that birds could do such daring things. Also, there is another bird that laughs loudly near lakes and in the dark forests. This bird calls to other friendly birds. Its voice says simply, "Loooo! Loooo! Looo!" And the friendly birds who are hiding answer back shouting,

"Loooo! Loooo! Loooo!"

Their voices quiver with excitement from finding a friend. These birds never get lost in the dark woods. Soon some of the birds in the school try to copy this sound. It seems like a good idea to keep from getting lost when traveling to strange places. At first only a few students softly say,

"Loooo! Loooo! Loooo!"

"Loooo! Loooo! Loooo!"

Soon, however, everyone in the class practices loudly shouting "LOOOO! LOOOO! LOOOO!"

Teacher Owl then says this bird is called the Loon. And the two-legged Birdmen think such a bird is crazy to make such a laughing sound. They laugh because they love to eat Veggies. The teacher is about to talk more, but class time was about to end. The school bell suddenly rings, but the birds did not want to leave. It was time to go.

"Teacher, tell us more! Tell us more!"

The students all shout together....The birds talk and laugh together.

"Cheep! Cheep! Cheep! Cheep! Cheep! Tweet! Tweet!"

"Veggies are good! Cheep! Cheep! Cheep! Cheep! Cheep!"

"Tweet! Tweet! Veggies are good! Looo! Looo! Looo!"

Students Sharing Favorite Veggies

This school is a happy place. A safe place. But it was time for the student birds to leave. The hot late afternoon sun is fading. Now it is time for the student birds to go home. Teacher Owl's head slowly spun around to show only the back of his head. No one could see his large dinner plate eyes go blinkity-blink.

Early in the afternoon the birds go home. Some students walk, some run, and others would try to fly if they can. Many young birds must go pass Rooster's Row where a line of older chickens ask them,

"What did you learn in school today?"

Some birds answer the big birds on Rooster's Row. Other students wait for their parents to ask questions when they are safe at home.

"What did you do today in school dear?"

Different voices express different answers:

"The Teacher taught us new things."

"We learned that some birds know how to catch and eat fish."

"We learned that some birds, I mean those Pigeons always beg."

"The Wise Owl, also said that after graduation most birds will go to work in *The Great Kitchen* forever."

"Some birds are not afraid of dogs that bark 'Bow Wow!' or 'Ruff Ruff!'"

"The Teacher said birds must adapt or die."

"Teacher said that there are Loony birds that can never get lost."

And many parents say to their young birds,

"Very good children. You were excellent when you pay attention in class. Now you may eat special cake crumbs for your delicious dessert. Then you must go to sleep early. Tomorrow will be another day for new adventures."

Also, that same evening, as Teacher Owl, now called "Big Eyes" by some birds, sat alone in the dark treetops. His mind was spinning in a slow circle. Perhaps in school he should tell the students his favorite secret. He was not sure if he should tell them, but he really wanted to tell them this special information.

Teacher Owl had learned that birds in the cities far away could drive buses. Teacher Owl knew this because he had two jobs. He worked as a Teacher in the daytime. And he works as a Listener-Watchman at night. He was a Moonlighter at night. At night he worries about sitting in the hot classroom with many birds. The heat inside the room makes his head spin around in slow circles.

Perhaps his students could help him solve this problem. It was too hot inside the classroom at school. That night when Wise Owl went to sleep, he only closes one eye. It may have been his yellow eye. Or, it may have been his blue eye. Who knows..? Hoot! Hoot! Whoooo!"

The Next day at school is very different. The sun shines with force and it is a very hot day. Teacher Owl talks about things that are dangerous to most birds. Again Brown Sparrow suggests,

"Let's go outside in the fresh air!"

"No, no!"

Said the guard, Rudy Rooster,

"You are too quick to fly off for food before learning anything new. You do not like to wait for the school bell to ring."

Teacher Owl continues to talk about Dangers. These are some of the things he said:

"Be careful where you walk. There may be snakes in the grass. Snakes like to bite and sting two-legged birdmen. But snakes also love to swallow birds. Little yellow chicks are tasty for snakes and alligators.

Sometimes alligators eat birds because they are tired of eating frogs. They like to change their diets."

The class made soft "Peep! Peep! Peep!" sounds. Such noises meant they were afraid to hear this news. Some birds covered their ears with their wings. They did not want to listen and know about dangerous things. These birds became so afraid they shivered. Their feathers shook and their bodies trembled.

But the Teacher said, "If you can sing the Happy Song, then you will not be afraid."

Teacher Owl began to sing:

"To be Happy and to know it, sing a song...

To be Happy and to know it sing a song..."

At this point someone interrupts the song. A loud voice says something which distracts students from singing. It is Chickee-Lickee-Lee.

"I THINK DOGS ARE A NUISANCE!"

Chickee-Lickee-Lee says this loudly.

"I agree!" Answers Brown Sparrow.

"Yes!! Yes!!" Coo the group of rooftop Pigeons lined up in a row. Dogs bark and say "ArF! ArF!" too much. They are noisy and have sharp teeth.

And then other birds offer complaints.

"Pigs are annoying too. They only say Oink! Oink! And they even eat meat!"

Many birds share a common fear:

"We are afraid to travel outside Paradise Farm because we do not know many safe places."

The entire class of birds groans in agreement. Thus, the students do not learn the Happy Song. Many birds begin chirping and tweeting all at once saying,

“Dogs chase us and pigs sometimes chase us too!”

A very small bird added,

“Two-legged people have big feet.”

Another bird says:

“Pigeons should not beg for food from two-legged people.”

“Dogs have four legs. We have no chance against them.”

“They will send us to *The Great Kitchen* before graduation.”

But the Pigeons had different opinions. The Pigeons have new information. They all speak at once making chirpy chatter and clamor.

“Four-legged creatures are not so annoying if you are quick on your feet. But you need to have three sharp toes on your feet.”

“We can easily get away from two-legs and four legs. We run fast, hop like rabbits, and also we can fly!”

“Well, well...” Teacher Owl interrupts the chatter.

“Since you can move quickly, then you must be related the Sandpiper bird. These small birds are found at windy beaches. They are extremely fast. These birds are small like skinny baby chicks. But their strong wings cut through stiff winds like a butter knife. I suppose the tiny toes of the Sandpiper bird help them to run as well as fly. One must learn to adapt or die.”

Chickee-Lickee-Lee is very quiet. She looks down, and a few tears drop on her foot with only two toes. Lucky for her no one notices. But what she has heard makes her feel hopeful of a happier future. Maybe someday she will no longer hop like a rabbit. Maybe someday her wings will grow strong enough to fly. Perhaps her feet would grow wide so she could paddle like a duck in the water. But she was still too young to know.

Then the Pigeons chime in cooing again.

"Yes, yes. But we hate bullies. Large, fat pigeons chase us away from bread crumbs and pizza slices on the ground. They are Bully Pigeons."

Another pigeon exclaims,

"Sometimes nice Bird Ladies and Birdmen try to feed us, but Bully Pigeons push us away. They take everything for themselves! We need Rudy Rooster in the parks to keep order."

"Yes. Yes! Yesss!" said many pigeons together at the same time.

Soon the classroom is noisy again. Birds are all chirping, tweeting, and happily laughing because this school is a safe place. But there are some funny rumors about Pinkie Pig whom they all know.

"Pinkie Pig thinks she is a two-legged human", says one bird.

They all laugh. "Ha ha ha ha ha!"

"She stands on her two hind legs and wears high heeled shoes!", says another.

The birds laughed again. "Ha ha ha hee hee!"

"Miss Pinkie Pig even wears dresses, necklaces and stuff. She is very funny to look at."

"Ha haha! Ha ha ha ha! Hee he ha ha!"

The birds in school chat noisily and Teacher Owl wisely listened. After a while when the noise died down close to silence, the Owl blinked his eyes at the class and says.

"So now that you are having fun, it is time for something serious."

But Duckee Duck challenges this point:

"What could be more serious than talking about a pig with four legs who walks on two feet?"

"Yes!", honked Goosey Loosey, sounding like a broken brass trumpet,

"Any pig standing tall wearing a dress is not natural. That's serious to me."

"Indeed! Indeed!"

Again all the birds chirp and tweet.

"Wel-l-l-l-l, Hoot! Hoot! Whooooo!" Teacher Owl bellows, "You must pay more attention. There are dangerous things all around you. There are also safe places to travel."

Teacher Owl tells the students about holes to hide in on tree trunks. He also mentions that strong new bird nests, if unoccupied, could be safe places. Shelter could be found under wide, thick leaves on plants. Especially, a bird can keep dry under leaves when it rains.

"Oh, but I like the rain", said Black Crow.

"I can stand in the rain on a wire and not fall."

"Ohhh, I see...", the Teacher Owl replies.

"You are strong and brave indeed. This is a good lesson class. Many of you have different skills to help you when traveling. Some of you can walk in groups in a straight line. Others of you can fly in groups like a feather cloud. Maybe, a few of you even can float in the pond water like a group of bouncy boats. These are good ways to travel to new areas, different places."

The Polly Blue Parrot announces a different topic. She says,

"I want to go to the city. I want to see little children playing in their houses. But many parrots can only go to these places if they are behind bars in metal cages."

Polly Red Parrot also agrees.

"Yes. I would like to travel to the city also, but I do not want to be a Jail Bird. Cages are prisons for many birds. This is not good."

"This is a Good point", said Teacher Owl.

"We all must obey rules for birds and avoid getting too close when two-legged people are around.

"We must learn to sing the Happy Song inside our heads. But, you must remember to adapt or die. Danger is on the ground where you walk. Deadly things are even in the air above you. You must beware. Do your homework. You should learn the Happy Song.

The chorus of birds groaned loudly.

"Awhhhh! Homework again!!!! Teacher tell us should we be afraid to walk? Must we fear flying in the air?"

Teaching Owl then said,

"To be Unafraid you must know this Happy Song. Let's try to sing it now. Okay?"

TO BE HAPPY YOU WILL KNOW IT... SING A SONG

To be happy you will know it, sing a song

You will never be afraid

You'll be strong and very brave

To be happy you can show it, sing a song!

That evening as the birds depart from the school a loud chorus of singing could be heard. These students are almost ready for graduation day. Soon they will be a little bigger, stronger, faster, and smarter. They will have more feathers on their wings. So, when you look around and see a bird flying happily, you will know this is a good student bird. And when you hear a bird singing merrily and whistling a tune, this is a happy bird.

Animals March singing Happy Song

//// THE END ////

FEATHERS IN THE SKIES

Farmers Confused by Falling Feathers

Today is a special day in the clouds. Not like any ordinary day, quiet and still. Shapes above the earth linger in the air like floating ghosts, ships, faces, wings. All seems okay. The sun is shining bright. The air feels pleasantly warm. Below the clouds, a few birds sing happily. Cheeping, twerping, tweeting, and chatting. Soft breezes make clouds drift lazily around in the sky shifting pictures. But today the clouds strangely look colorful like balloons. Reds, mixed with greens, yellows, and blue colors. The clouds are no longer gray and white. They have festive colors. Vibrant rainbows.

Nobody is working today. No birds are flying high in the skies. No hunters are looking for food. Even below the clouds nothing moves. Four-legged animals and two-legged fathers, mothers, sisters, and brothers are sleeping. But something is not right. The colors of the clouds should have been a clue. But two-legged people are not looking at clouds. Most human eyes are closed sleeping. Dreaming. Most humans like sleeping better than anything else.

But, a few families who do wake up early become unhappy. Men and women start to argue about small matters. On this strange morning, they frown at each other. They do not sweetly say “Good Morning.” Instead, they shout angry words and complain about the sky.

Clouds unhappy eating feathers

However, the colorful clouds had full stomachs which made them also unhappy. It was not water, cold ice, or snow filling a cloud's stomach. Strangely their meals had become colorful. Today, the clouds above Paradise Farms were neither hungry nor thirsty. Today, all of the clouds were lazy and grumpy. They were not in the mood to think about making any rain. This is what healthy clouds usually did. Clouds made rain or snow. But not these days.

Mighty wind sometimes blew a little stronger. Then more colors fell from the clouds. What were those colors? Where did they come from? Something unusual had happened.

?@@? GUESS WHY SO MANY COLORS WERE AROUND? !@@!

Yes, this was a great mystery. Some creatures guessed this is what happened: An early bird was flying above the treetops. Suddenly this bird began losing a few feathers. One, two, and then three feathers fell from this flying body. Usually, these feathers were not important. Birds lose feathers all the time. That is why chickens on the ground do not get lost because they follow fallen feathers. Feathers can become clues like markers to help birds find paths back home.

Chickee Lee Discovers Naked birds

However, today the bird that was flying high soon lost more feathers from his wings. These were important feathers. His wings became thinner and thinner. With less feathers his wings could no longer help the motor keeping him in the air. So this bird began to fly lower and lower. He did not want to go lower. But he had no important feathers on his body to keep him up. Also feathers on his body were his clothes keeping him warm. So now his cold trembling body fell closer and closer to the ground. Lucky for him he was able to land on his feet when he touched the ground.

But this was just one surprise. The other surprise was that when his feet touched the ground he had no feathers on his body at all. He looked like a strange skinny thing. So weird. He wears no clothes. He is actually naked. He looked so funny that he laughs at himself.

"Twitter-twitter-twitter! Tweet-tweet- tweet!"

Laughing again and again. Soon he was called a "Naked Jay-Bird". He wears no feather clothes. He had nothing on his wings. Nothing covering his body. At first, other birds laugh with him, but later they will not be laughing at all.

Soon, other birds, large or small, plain, or very colorful, began to lose their feathers. This happens when they flew above the tree lines. When they fly high these birds also became skinny and naked. So they stop laughing. They also stop singing. No one wants to fly anymore. Without feathers birds could not keep warm. Most importantly, with no wing feathers, birds could no longer fly. Staying on the ground many birds are getting lost. Also, many birds are becoming easy meals for the hungry four-legged creatures with big teeth. This is not good.

?@@? Can you imagine where those loose bird feathers were going?@@?

Loose feathers began to float and collect in small bunches. Loose feathers from those unfortunate birds were causing a big problem. Clouds normally eat and drink soft things. And because the important bird feathers were lingering in the air and floating up higher, clouds became curious. Soon clouds began to eat tasty bird feathers. This was a delicious dish. Feathers tasted so sweet. Younger clouds could not stop eating feathers. Clouds would hum "Yummy! Yummy!" Making soft pleasant sounds. "Hummm. Yummy! Yummie!...Hummm!" It was not like thunder. Not scary sounding at all.

Soon feather stuffed clouds touching other hungry clouds became sick. They began to cough and spit. Larger clouds became so full they started choking. Their faces were turning dark because they could not breathe. Soon their faces were also darker with anger.

Although the clouds were becoming full of white feathers, gray feathers, and colorful feathers... their faces were red, and sometimes dark purple. The clouds were full. Not with water. Not with ice or snow. The clouds were stuffed with feathers. Clouds could not breathe properly. Clouds could not make rain. Clouds could not make snow. Only feathers began to float down when strong winds blew. More feathers began to fall to the ground from high-flying birds. This problem touched birds that flew high for many months and years.

Things were not good with bird feathers floating loose in the air filling clouds. Fat clouds in the air were becoming fatter. Thin, flimsy clouds were becoming dark and thick. Even below on the ground some animals were beginning to react to the changes. Birds on the ground were no longer singing. This became especially noticeable around 4:00 a.m. Early mornings when cats began howling as if their tails were on fire. Ducks angrily quacked. Roosters crowed without stopped for rest.

"Raaaah! Raaaah! RAAAAHHH!"A dog somewhere barked, "Shut up! Arf!"

But cats continue to scream and whine.

"Meowwww! Raaah! RAAAAHHH! YEOWWW!"

Then more farmers wake up. A husband starts to argue with his wife. Their voices become loud. Tom-cats continue to screech and whine. And more dogs far and near are barking.

"Ruff! Ruff! Shut up! Ruff! Ruff! Ruff!"

But the two Tom-cats continued to whine.

"Raaahhh! REE-ooow! Raaahhh! REE-OOOW!"

The voice of the farmer's wife now was tearful. Her crying words could be heard above the dog and cat noise.

"Why are the clouds so dark? We have no rain! Why? Why? Oh why?"

Soon she was throwing her shoes against the barn wall hoping to quiet the noises outside.

"Thump! Thump!"

Two shoes hit the wall. Then one of the farmers' heavy boots came next.

"Boomp!"

Husband and Wife Farmers Unhappy

These noises arouse all the farm animals from their deep slumber. The horses neigh, pigs oink, and cows moow. Even after being milked the cows continue making noises.

"Moow! Moow! Moooooow!"

These noises caused the bird voices to raise in nervous chatter. It was like a wild carnival of sounds.

"Kerperrr! Kerperrr!"

“Cluck-Cluck! Cluck-Cluck!”

“Cock-a-doodle-doo! Cock-a-doodle-doooo!”

Chattering. Mooing. Cackling. Barking. Whining. Jeeez! This was a terrible problem! Trouble. Feathers choking clouds in the sky were causing many problems below on the farm. No one could sleep. Some would say this was all a big mystery. Everyone has questions. But no one had answers. Somebody needs to help. But Who?

However, this is what we do know. For one thing, yesterday, and the day before yesterday, and the day before the day before yesterday, fateful things had started to happen. Each day the air became harmed by poisons. Poisons are tiny germs no eyes can see. These poisons are created by fumes and chemicals when humans burn things. Fires burn things. Fires from factories push black smoke into the air. Exhaust fumes from fast automobiles send harmful poisons into the air. Careless campers using fires in forests also cause innocent trees to burn. Many trees are lost. Thick gray and black smoke sends invisible poisons into the air

A few two-legged people had been burning tall trees by accident. More two-legged workers at Paradise Farm, smoking cigarettes, coughed while laughing. These two-legged people were called “Chain-Smokers”. Day and night they could not stop smoking. They kept little white paper sticks in their mouths. Some forgetful people kept burning sticks hanging loosely from their lips. Forgotten. They did not remember those sticks were in their mouths. This only added to the air quality problems.

Chickee-Lee Questions featherless birds

Green Leaf waddles like a duck from one leg to the other. But Green Leaf is not a duck. He is a Parrot. The ground feels strange and wonderful. It feels like sailing on a cloud. He imagines that he is floating, not walking. All three toes on each of his feet are touching on the ground. How can this be? He is thinking. People say that birds ride buses in human cities. Some feathered creatures are even called King Fisher birds. They dive deep into the water and easily catch fish. And Wise Owls are known to actually drive human buses. They drive buses carrying children to school. Imagine that!

These may have only been fake stories. Rumors. But this new feeling of walking on a soft pillow is strange indeed. This is no rumor. Green Leaf Parrot cannot feel the earth beneath his feet. The earth is soft and springy. He bounces on the path home. Bouncing feels good. He is smart. He is also proud that his green feathers shine in the sunlight. His feathers are beautiful. This is why Green Leaf Parrot is a good name for him. He wears his name well.

"Did you see what he did? "Did you see what that Parrot did?

Two brown featherless Sparrows chirp to each other. They are watching Green Leaf. The Parrot waddles across the road. He then hops on a wire cage that protects other parrots. Through a small hole in the cage he gingerly steps. Green Leaf is now inside the cage. Then he turns upside down and crawls like a lizard with his back facing the ground.

"Did you see that?"

But the two brown Sparrows do not look like the birds they once had been. Their mistake earlier was to fly above the treetops. Now they were naked. They both have no feathers and look like two tiny brown mice or dusty moles. They huddle near the open mouth of a small hole in the ground. Since they cannot fly without feathers, they are trying to seek shelter in holes in the earth. This was risky because any hole might be home to dangerous scorpions with sharp claws and stingers. **A naked bird is a very scared bird**. A hole could be a home for rabbits with large sharp teeth. Worse, a hole could be home to a long, thick snake ready to bite or swallow an intruder. Or perhaps it was only a small Gopher hole.

"Did you see that? A green Parrot so smart and nimble. Wow!"

The two featherless Sparrows were so stunned watching Green Leaf the Parrot, they forgot to watch the hole behind them. Something dangerous had slithered out and is close to their heads. This is not a Gopher.

"Look out! Look out! Birrrrddddd!"

Green Leaf Parrot squawks a warning to the brown featherless birds. But it is too late. With one gulp, the wide-open mouth of a thick Shiney Snake sucked the birds. Suddenly, they disappear like magic into the mouth and down his long tunnel throat.

“Ahh! That was delicious!” The Shiney Snake burps a sound of satisfaction and disappears back into his hole in the ground.

“Oh my Gawd! I shouted ‘look out!’ but those two birds did not listen. They were too slow. I must go to the *Council of High-Flying Birds* and report this new danger to featherless birds.”

Featherless birds are easy victims

However, leaders of the *Council of High-Flying Birds* are very, very big strong birds. Eagles, Falcons, Hawks, a Fighting Rooster, and one King Fisher bird. They are the largest of the large birds. They were not afraid of snakes. And they have not lost feathers like smaller birds. Twice a year very large birds like these lose only four feathers. It is normal to lose one feather from each wing in the spring, and one from each wing in the autumn. Rare feathers from large birds are treasures to humans. Two-legged humans valued highly feathers from very large birds.

Leaders of the *Council of High-Flying Birds* are not concerned about the problem Green Leaf Parrot squawks about. As far as these very large birds are concerned, losing feathers is natural. Furthermore, to very large birds, smaller birds have no business flying above treetops anyway. The sky areas above the treetops are off-limits to them.

Years ago, Wise Owls had been commissioned to spread this policy far and wide. So, if there are disobedient birds flying above the treetops, they deserve to be punished. As far as very large birds are concerned, colorful feathers on the ground were not a bad thing. Naked birds trying to hide in holes for mice is not their concern. The large birds simply turn cold-eyed stares at the squawking Parrot. In their minds, the world is moving okay. Fat clouds with feathers instead of water is of no interest to big birds.

Adult Birds Ponder the farm Air problem

Even the long-necked white swans who swam lazily all day on lakes and ponds, are not alarmed about birds who lose feathers. Swans never flew very high anyway. It is against their rules. Most of their time was spent romantically with their partners cruising on waterways. Swans have not lost any feathers. Thus, they side with the Eagles, Falcons, and Hawks. They have the same opinion as the very large birds: smaller birds should not fly above treetops. Feathers lost by birds flying too high is punishment for disobeying a proper rule set by the Special Council of Birds.

Today, the Council of High-Flying Birds are in a special private meeting. Guarding the old Wood Mill doorway hung Batty Gray Bat. He has no feathers, but he can also fly high. He does not pretend to sleep during the daytime. He is asleep, upside down. It is easy for him to catch flying insects who try entering the old Wood Millhouse. The hook-like claws on Bat wing elbows allow for peaceful rest, upside down, wherever and whenever they choose. However, behind closed doors at the old Wood Mill, the very large birds of the Council are having a loud discussion. It is their view that too many smaller birds had disobeyed the policy to not fly above tree lines.

Wise Owl is trying to focus his mind. His large rolling saucer eyes blink rapidly. He thinks there are too many causes making the clouds become filled with feathers.

"I'll say it again, when years ago I heard the Red Robins training their young to sing I knew that this would cause problems. I knew it!"

"How can you be so sure," quipped a large Turkey Buzzard. He stretches his crooked neck as three large walnuts moved up and down inside his skinny throat. Two long wiry hairs on his shrunken chin stand out straight.

"Those small red birds are not the only birds that sing you know."

As he speaks his neck looks more like a crooked letter "Z" in a knot. The walnut lumps inside his neck rattle and shake. His neck does not become straight even when he swallows rotten meat. But now he just made an important point.

"You are correct, Turkey Buzzard, indeed there are other birds that sing. But the Red Robins train their young to sing these words:

'FLY ROBINS FLY! FLY ROBINS FLY! ROBINS FLY... UP, UP TO THE SKY!!

Of course, the red feathers on the ground have been falling from the stuffed clouds. There can be no doubt about this. When they fly up high, they soar above the treetops. This is against our policy rules."

Now, Gregory Goose, the representative for the Long Necked Canadian Geese, interjects his opinion.

"Well, we fly high when going south, even above the clouds, but going through those clouds stuffed with feathers we have also seen blue feathers, and yellow feathers. So, obviously, the smaller red robins are not the only culprits breaking our policies. Parrots perhaps also should be blamed."

"True, true", said Wise Owl, "the Blue Birds, Yellow Swallows, and mixed colored Parrots may all be equally at fault. Proof is the evidence of blue and yellow feathers also on the ground. Red feathered birds are not the only rule breakers."

Old Baldy Eagle, the council chairman, is clearly bored with this discussion. Disobedient birds get what they deserve. Small boastful birds should lose their feathers. This is nature's punishment. His eyes remain cold and the lines around his sharp mouth are firm and stern. He is always very serious. He remains quiet. He closes his eyes and leans his head against the barn mill wall. Above his head was a placard that has seven words in bold black print:

"WE AIR POLICE TAKE WHAT WE WANT!"

This is a slogan all council members repeat before starting each meeting.

Hermit Hawk is quiet. Hermit Hawk is thinking about rabbits he will swoop down from the clouds and catch with his sharp talons. His movements are lightning-fast and silent. He loves the sweet taste of rabbit meat. He also loves the taste of small birds too. Naked birds without feathers to fly are now easier to catch.

He stands in silence filing his toenails so they become sharper than a butcher's meat knife. He does not care to talk about small birds that sing. He does not care about feathers of any color in the sky or on the ground. His wings will always be strong. He has not lost feathers because he does not want to lose feathers. In fact, it is a simple matter to catch a naked Jay Bird that stumbles around looking for a place to hide. Chasing birds in the sky is simply too much work. But these thoughts are interrupted by another voice.

"I think we should do a survey! We could count the different colors of feathers on the ground."

"What? A survey? Who are you?" Demanded Baldy Eagle opening his steely eyes. His huge wings do not move.

"I am Chickee-Lickee-Lee. Many animals and birds laugh at me because I only have two toes. I fly only a little but not very high. Perhaps you will also laugh at me. But, I know a way to find out what kind of birds are flying above the tree lines. I might be able to determine why only certain birds lose feathers. I want to help solve this problem. Please give me a chance."

"Wait just a minute. How did you get inside this meeting place? This is a private meeting only for large birds! You should leave immediately!"

Baldy Eagles' face and eyes reflected a fierce stubborn resolve. No patience. No smile. He fixes his stare off into a faraway place. However, Chickee-Lickee-Lee tries to brave this resistance and continues.

"I..I.. I am sorry. I will leave if my assistance is not needed. I thought I could help by getting you useful information."

"Listen little Chickee what-ever-your-long-name is, we really do not need your advice," snaps Baldy Eagle. "You cannot fly above the treetops, so stay out of big bird business! By the way, you are not allowed in this meeting anyway. No Chickens are allowed. That is policy."

Four large heads of powerful bird Council, stare intently down at very small Chickee-Lickee-Lee. She tightly clutches her Mystery Gadget. They intend to intimidate and scare her away.

Group Intimidation

"That's right" chimes Hermit the Hawk, as he pauses from filing his sharp toe-claws. "If you do not disappear quickly, I may have to change my meal plans this evening. Then there will be one less chicken for farmers to count. A few more feathers on the ground are not going to hurt anyone. I can easily forget my diet. Maybe someone will even stuff pillows with your yellow fluff."

The Hawk's wings twitch ready to pounce.

“Ha! Counting feathers is a weak idea.” Spat Turkey Buzzard trying to stretch his crooked neck. The two wiry hairs on his chin waved frantically. One sunken hooded eye remains half closed.

“A two-toed yellow chicken is useless. I remember the time...”

But Wise Owl intervenes. As an old teacher, he recognizes his former student, the small two-toed chicken he had taught basic flying techniques months ago. The Owl speaks with urgency.

“Well, we must start by doing something. Don’t be cruel to the child. This is a special chicken. In pastimes this bird has proven a valuable resource when we had problems at *Paradise Farm*. I am curious. Let’s give her a chance. Let’s hear her ideas. Are you okay with this?”

But Pelican Pete, who usually was silent spoke up.

“No... No... No!”

And Randy the Black Raven let out a loud stream of interruptions: “NEVER MORE! NEVER MORE! NEVER MORE!”

Actually, although Randy Raven Is a very large crow, he was not an official member of the Bird Council. He Is never allowed to vote or make decisions. But he had a habit of sticking his sharp black beak, smooth head, and beady red eyes through the old Wood Mill’s broken roof. He just does not have enough nerve to enter the door that Batty Gray Bat guards. Randy Raven is not brave enough to enter the room. Thus, the council of birds ignore his noisy words.

Pelican Pete continues.

“We must continue our long-held policies. Must I remind you that WE ARE THE AIR POLICE? It does not matter whether some creatures think our rules are good or bad, a policy is a policy. That’s a fact!”

“Will you please kindly explain yourself?” asked Wise Owl. “What do you mean saying long held policies are facts? Policies are not facts, they are rules.”

“What I really mean” said Pelican Pete, “is this: Policies govern our lives. Rules keep our society balanced and harmonious. For example: Rule #1- Two-legged creatures called ‘humans’ are our natural enemies; Rule #2- Four-legged creatures who cannot speak clearly should be working beasts for humans; Rule #3- High-flying birds deserve complete freedom; Rule #4- Areas above the tree tops, cliffs, and mountain peaks are only reserved for large strong birds; and finally, Rule #5- Birds that produce eggs in a bountiful manner should be allowed a life of choice: Chicken coop security, or risky free-ranging.”

Turkey Buzzard mumbles to himself. His crooked neck moves again in a strange manner.

“We have always told those birds to fly low. They do not. This really is not our problem.”

There was a brief moment of silence. Several seconds pass with no one speaking. Then another bird chirps.

“Well, perhaps... just perhaps” advises Suzie Swan, “a new change is in order. Maybe we should add a new policy? Think about it. We could forbid birds to not train their young to sing. No more singing. And then, with no singing those birds will not even think about flying high where we large birds fly. We swans do not sing. We Swans like to make horn-honking sounds. Honks are better than singing. Singing is not good for one’s health.”

“Ah yes! A Healthy throat is important,” croaked Rooster Rodman. He serves on the Council as honorary member.

“How can I wake everyone up every morning if my throat hurts?”

He had a very sharp beak, long, sharp claws on his toes, and dangerous hooks at the back of his feet. His red hunting cap wiggles as he continues speaking.

"It is also important that we preserve the policies of this Council. Chickens must always be reminded that they have freedom. They can roam around hunting and pecking for seeds and cold worms. But if preferred, they can remain safely penned up in Hen Houses sitting on warm eggs. I watch over chickens. That's my job."

"Or, chickens can live their lives in Zoos like captive prisoners!" Interrupts Turkey Buzzard. "Chickens should realize they have good lives, they never work hard. They can retire in *The Great Kitchen* to rest in peace. In my opinion, they are more useful than pigeons. Retirement for birds is a good thing. A very good thing."

But Chickee-Lickee-Lee is quick to debate these comments saying,

"The problem is not birds singing. All birds do not sing the same songs that Red Robins sing. And the problem is not about Chickens. Feathers are not falling from all types of birds. Just the other day... when...a colorful parrot...."

The little yellow chicken's words were cut off by Pelican Pete.

"What you think does not matter. You are a chicken, your life is to either lay eggs, or roam around in a lazy life until you become too bored with your neighbors. You are free to retire anytime to *The Great Kitchen*. Phew! You have no real worries."

Wise Owl, however, quickly realizes they are not solving the main problem. Personal attacks on the small yellow bird, are not helpful. Wise Owl also knows from past experiences the little yellow chicken had a magical brain, a smart mind. He has seen this yellow chicken speak to a crying lion. Before this had been rumors that Chickee-Lickee-Lee also had spoken to a hungry bear. And long, long ago the forest leaves held whispers of hearing this same chicken talking to a potato. None of this had been confirmed, but perhaps the yellow bird could prove useful for handling the cloud problem. He could only hope. So, he speaks his mind.

"Listen, a little input from a small one closer to the ground will not hurt us. Let's pause for a few minutes and listen to someone new. Okay? Whoooo wants to hear what this little yellow chicken wants to say? Whoooo is not in a hurry? Whoooo is curious about all those colorful feathers everywhere? Let's take a vote on hearing Chickee-Lickee-Lee's voice on this matter."

Baldy Eagle shifts on his perch. His mouth tightens in a stern line. He stretches his huge wings to balance himself. A strong aroma of wood pine circulated in the air around him. He looks at Wise Owl's large saucer eyes. Wise Owl's head slowly rotated spinning in a circle. Then Baldy Eagle fastens his stare at Henry the Hawk who sits close to Frannie Falcon. There are nine important members of the *Council of High-Flying Birds*. This odd number means that if the vote is not unanimous, a tie-breaker would be needed. Baldy Eagle was ready to agree.

"Fine. Let's vote. And since I am chairman, I will vote last. Go ahead. Let those who do not want to hear the little yellow chicken talk, answer when your name is called. Lift one wing to say Yes, or to not move means No."

Outside the Old Barn Millhouse, where the bird council had gathered, are other listening ears. Four-legged farm animals listen. Pigeons lined up on telephone wires listen. Brown sparrows, and black crows, tweet, chirp, and are listening. Smaller birds remained hidden among branches and leaves. A few birds are loudly chanting. Some hold printed signs.

"STOP STEALING FEATHERS!"

"STOP STEALING FEATHERS!!"

But these voices could not be heard by the bird council inside the Old Barn Millhouse. Protest signs are not seen. The large sleeping Gray Batty Bat hanging upside down over the doorway entrance, flutters his wings several times when each name is called.

Wise Owl starts the roll call. The Council of Birds begins voting on a decision to listen, or not to listen, to Chickee-Lickee-Lee's plan. Many older birds want to ignore the subject regarding the loss of bird feathers. The following names are called:

Rooster Rodman - "Yes"

Frannie Falcon - "No"

Hermit Hawk - "No"

King Fisher bird - "No"

Pelican Pete - "No"

Suzie Swan - "No"

Gregory Goose - "Yes"

Turkey Buzzard - "No"

Wise Owl - "Yes"

Baldy Eagle - "No"

Farm Creatures Overhear Noisy Barn Meeting

“Okay. That’s it. The votes are in. And now we can move on.” Says chairman Baldy Eagle, his steely gaze fixed on a distant point. No need to prolong the obvious. Goodbye little chicken. Try not to wake-up Batty the Gray Bat as you go out the door.”

The Eagle’s voice did not sound kind. Other birds make unkind comments.

"Goodbye yellow ball, don't hop into any accidents with those tiny toes of yours. Try to be more balanced. Ha... ha! The real world is quite different than you small birds can imagine. Ha...ha...ha! You have no idea! Ha.. ha.. ha...ha...he...he... he!"

Most of the other large birds joined in the laughter. But Wise Owl and Rooster Rodman keep silent. Chickee-Lickee-Lee departs quietly. However, as she passes Batty the Gray Bat, he swings at her head with one hook on his wing. His open red mouth reveals two sharp snake-like fangs. He hisses and flutters his wings as if to pounce on the chicken. In a split second Chickee-Lickee-Lee bounds away with surprising speed. With a half hop and two wings flapping she settles on a tree branch close by.

Randy Raven is perched on the roof edge of the Old Mill barn. The Raven winks one red eye at the nervous Chickee-Lickee-Lee. The Raven loudly warns: ''NEVER MORE! NEVER MORE!''

Inside the Old Mill Barn more bird conversations can be heard.

"I just don't get it" said Susie Swan. "Why would we bother taking a survey? Counting colors of different feathers on the ground would be meaningless."

"Well, as I see it," retorted Hermit Hawk, "that yellow chicken is the problem. I think that anyone who challenges our policies and rules must be closely watched."

"Agreed. Agreed." Said Pelican Pete, "That chicken broke our rule coming to this private meeting. Ignoring the 'No Chickens Allowed' policy is a clear sign she is a Trouble-Maker. Someone must teach her a new lesson. Our rules must be obeyed."

Baldy Eagle blinks his steely gray eyes once and partly opens his sharp beak.

"Yes... yes... perhaps we should cause that mischievous chicken to seek early retirement."

Wise Owl quickly agrees. He does not want anyone to feel that he cares for the chicken. Afterall, many large birds enjoy snacking on chicken meat for meals. Also, that he has been teaching Chickee-Lickee-Lee flying tips is a well-kept secret.

"Fine idea! Excellent! I shall immediately recommend her to the staff workers at *The Great Kitchen."*

But Suzie Swan remembers the issue of feathers on the ground. And Gregory Goose remembers struggling through bulging clouds stuffed with feathers. Flying against strong winds was easy compared to fighting through thick colorful clouds filled with feathers. The problem they had been alerted about by Green Leaf Parrot has not been solved. Suzie Swan finally voices her concern.

"So, Chairman Eagle, how are we going to handle birds who insist on teaching their young to sing, and fly high above treetops? We need to take a tough stand otherwise there will always be feathers in the clouds."

"And let me add this," interjects Gregory Goose. We still have not identified the cause of feathers becoming stuck in the clouds. We need to know the primary cause. We cannot guarantee a solution without a complete investigation."

****

Far into the evening the *Council of High-Flying Birds* discusses many issues. Baldy Eagle, the Chairman, simply dozes in and out of sleep. Wise Owl continues writing notes so every member can participate fairly. He urges them to remember they must be dutiful police of the airways.

"Frankly, let's face it. There are just too many birds and too many chickens."

Then a King Fisher bird makes this suggestion:

“Perhaps it is good that weak birds stay out of the sky. We have never lost our feathers flying high. The old saying is very true: ‘Only the strong survive’. Now we have enough proof.”

“Birds sing too much anyway. We need quietness. Hunters appreciate the stillness and calm. Silent birds have a natural sense. However, loud-singing birds are careless and not considerate of the needs of others. I say, let’s drop the matter. No investigation is required.”

King Fisher birds prefer diving into cold water to catch fresh juicy fish. Hunting flying creatures, or chasing other birds is not attractive to him or his friends.

Soon Wise Owl did not have enough paper to keep writing notes. The Bird Council was not close to creating a plan. But Wise Owl knows many things. His grandparents, mother, father, and cousins have been car and bus drivers. Some have helped humans fiddling with numbers doing tax accounting work. It also was known to him that humans have used Canary birds in the precious silver and coal mines to test for air safety. Tiny Canary birds had been put in cages to test the air deep in the earth. Perhaps these same birds could be useful for tests in the clouds. Again, Wise Owl speaks his mind.

“Are we not the Air Police?”

“Wh...wh.. whaaaat? What are you talking about?”

The members of the *Council of Those Who Fly High* are suddenly hushed into silence. In only a few minutes the Wise Owl launched his plan for a new investigation.

“But... how are we to catch a Canary?”

Council members are perplexed, especially Frannie Falcon and Hermit Hawk.

"The plan sounded good until you suggested putting a Canary in a cage. The Canary is a tiny bird. So small and very weak. It's body is fragile like thin glass. Usually, if we catch one, it is no longer breathing. Their tiny hearts stop beating."

"Yes, they die in the air from fright."

"And you expect one of us to carry a heavy metal cage with a live Canary up into the clouds. Humpf! That's ridiculous!"

"Not ridiculous.... foolish. That's a stupid idea!"

Frannie Falcon and Hermit Hawk believe that using a Canary for testing clouds will not work. But Old Baldy Eagle can see the practicality of this plan. He is much stronger than the two complaining birds. Using a heavy metal cage will not bother him. However, a new question to Wise Owl disturbs his keen mind.

Flying Eagle and Cage

“Listen, Wise Owl, I want to know is it necessary to only use a Canary? Is there another type of bird that can be useful for cloud testing?”

Wise Owl slowly responded.

"Well-l-l-l-l the Hummingbird could be useful. They are quite small and not heavy. It would be easy to carry a Canary into the clouds. However, they are too fast for any of us to catch."

Turkey Buzzard agrees.

"So very true. They are too fast and their hearts are weak. We need a brave bird with a very strong heart. Only large birds have strong hearts for this task, but a strong-hearted bird is much too heavy to carry in a cage for testing."

"We must think of another plan."

****

CAN YOU GUESS WHAT HAPPENS NEXT?

****

Chickee-Lickee-Lee tries to steady herself as the cage rocks back and forth. The higher the Eagle flies the winds ferociously rattle the wooden cage bars. Wood is not heavy like metal. The yellow chicken looked at the shiny detective badge a bird council member had pinned onto her shirt. The past events were not a dream. She was not assigned to *The Great Kitchen*. Instead, she had been chosen to investigate the clouds. It was now her official job to discover why the clouds are eating feathers. Clouds stopped producing water, ice, and snow. Bird feathers are being stuck in clouds or falling to the earth.

But Chickee-Lickee-Lee is not alone. Also inside the wooden cage with her is the very small Red Leaf Parrot. The *Council of High-Flying Birds* wants the parrot to be a witness to whatever happens in the clouds.

A parrot had started the rumors about falling feathers. It was fitting that if there was to be an end to gossip, a parrot should be a witness, for good or for bad.

Strong Baldy Eagle carries the cage higher. The two birds in the cage can hardly breathe. Soon they were far above the pine treetops. The pleasant smells from flowers and trees are no longer detected. In a few seconds, they will enter the thick dark clouds full of colorful feathers. There will be no smells at all. Soon they no longer see the distant earth below. Feathers of all colors were everywhere. Sounds of clouds coughing could be heard by the birds in the cage. Chickee-Lickee-Lee looks at Red Leaf Parrot who is shivering near her.

“Are you all right little parrot? Are you coughing?”

“No! I am not all right! I am cold! But I am not coughing. Perhaps it is the old eagle who is tired from carrying this heavy cage.”

Then Chickee-Lickee-Lee shouts at the eagle who effortlessly flaps his wings through the thick colorful clouds.

“Baldy Eagle are you coughing? Are you all right?”

“Of course, I am all right. No, I am not coughing.”

“Well, we hear coughing. Perhaps it is time for us to return to the ground. This investigation seems fruitless.”

The Exhausted Bird Rests on the Magic "Gizmo"

But the Eagle is strong. His few remarks are firm.

"Do your job little bird! Do your investigation! Do not be weak! This is not a vacation trip!"

The Eagle's voice is so loud and stern that the clouds begin to tremble. Then another voice isheard in the distance. But only Chickee-Lickee-Lee hears this new voice.

"Hello! Hello! Is somebody new disturbing us today? What are you doing here?"

Baldy Eagle does not speak much when carrying the cage in his mouth. In fact, he does not understand Cloud language. He only speaks bird language. Most birds only spoke to birds. However, Chickee-Lickee-Lee can speak to rocks and veggies. She also talks to animals. Actually, it was magic that she could also understand words coming from the clouds.

"Hello back! Who are you? Are you coughing?"

"Yes, we clouds are suffering from being thirsty. Poisons from fires and human engines make us addicted to feathers. We cannot taste moisture in the air."

"How do you know that poisons humans make cause you to be thirsty?"

"How do we know? HOW DO WE KNOW? We can smell the exhaust from factories. We can smell the fumes from automobiles and trucks. We can smell the choking smoke from forest fires. If you lived up high as we do, you would smell these terrible things too!"

/////////////////////

NO ONE can say Chickee-Lickey-Lee is bad or irresponsible. All the residents at Paradise Farms know that she is helpful, caring, and responsible. She is a bird with special qualities. And any chicken with special qualities should not be trained for *The Great Kitchen*. Maybe, such a chicken should be protected. Perhaps.

Do you agree?

And Chickee-Lickee-Lee also had two secrets.

Can you guess what her first secret was?

The first big secret is that she had a good brain.

Do you know what a brain is?

Where is your brain?

Some people say that big brains are smart, and little brains are not smart.

Some people say birds have small brains and this means they are not smart.

Big brain creatures make jokes when a person makes a mistake. They laugh and say, "That was a mistake, you must only have a birdbrain!"

"Birds are so stupid!"

Do you know that a brain is a computer inside the bird's head? Yes, the brain is a precious machine inside a bird's head.

Chickee-Lickee-Lee also had a second secret.

The second important secret this chicken had was her resourcefulness. She remembered to use her brain to think. She remembered that a brain is not just for choosing food. A brain is not only for eating. A brain is not just for remembering words and singing songs. A brain is not used only for playing games. And most importantly, a brain is not only for dreaming.

Do you know where a chicken keeps its brain?

So, can you tell me what else a brain can be used for? Do you know?

Well, let us not forget a happy bird is a good student. To be a happy bird one must use a brain to have a good memory. Chickee-Lickee-Lee was a happy bird. That is to say, she always remembers to bring her favorite toy wherever she travels.

Yes, Chickee-Lickee-Lee had a favorite toy.

Can you guess what her favorite toy is?

Her toy was a Smart Digital Watch.

Do you know where she wears her favorite toy?

**** ****

But she does not wear the *Smart Digital Watch* on her arm like human people. She wears her watch on her best leg. This way it is easy to take it off and put it away in her toy box. This *Smart Digital Watch* has four functions. It works because of sunlight. This light is solar power.

Now that she is high in the sky the *Smart Digital Watch* tells her four things:

1. You are flying too high or too Low [White light steady or blinking]
2. You are going too Fast or Too Slow [Yellow light blinking- or not blinking]
3. Your air visibility is a thick cloud or thin cloud means easy or difficult to see straight ahead
4. Air Quality Dangerous is at levels: Danger = RED buzzer, or No Danger = Green Light flashes.

Now up in the sky with *the Strong Eagle, things begin to happen.*

All the lights on her Smart Digital Watch are rapidly blinking. All lights blink except the RED light.

Even from the machine in the cage lights are blinking. These were warning lights.

Chickee-Lickee-Lee hears strange noises coming from the machine box.

She heard warning sounds,

"Beep-Beep-Be-eep!"

"Beep-Beep-Be-eep!"

Chickee-Lickee-Lee again looks her *Smart Digital Watch*. The flashing Red and Yellow lights told her they were in dangerous air zones. The Great Eagle also hears strange noises.

"Beep-Beep-Be-eep!"

The Eagle is surprised. He growled at Chickee-Lickee-Lee.

"What are you doing? Why are you making these strange sounds? You are supposed to be testing the clouds? DO YOUR JOB! HURRY UP!"

The Eagle shouts angrily. He wants to quickly fly back home with a simple report.

However, Chickee-Lickee-Lee ignores his words. Her eyes stare at the magic box in the cage that is testing the air. The arrow on the dial's face points to danger. Gasoline fumes from airplanes are poison. This smell is also deadly to anyone who sniffs the exhaust from engines.

Finally, Chickee-Lickee-Lee knows what to do. She immediately knows why birds are losing their feathers. Hearing her words the Eagle's wings beat stronger. The birdcage moves faster in the air.

Chickee-Lickee-Lee Examines Safety "Gizmo"

"We can go home now. I know what the problem is. I will write a report to the Animal Council at Paradise Farms. Let's go home!"

Soon they safely land back on the ground. The residents are amazed to see that the Chicken did not lose any feathers. Chickee-Lickee-Lee immediately goes home to prepare her report. The animals chat among themselves. They even try to make Baldy Eagle tell them a few secrets about the sky and clouds. But he will not. He does not open his mouth. He never even smiles. So, they must wait. Many birds are impatient. They keep disturbing the Chicken and the Eagle. They make many chattering, honking, and clucking sounds. You know how noisy birds can be. They interrupt each other frequently.

"Is it done yet?"

"Is it done yet?"

"Please tell us what you know. It is unfair to keep secrets. We want to fly as high as possible, too, you know."

"Tell us something. It's almost time for dinner."

Finally, Chickee-Lickee-Lee goes to the Wise Owl at the meeting house. She is ready to share her important information. She explains why the skies and clouds are filled with bird feathers. This is what she says:

"Ladies and gentlemen, we all have heard that Geese who fly high get strike airplanes and die. Or they get stuck in airplane engines and die.

We also know that for years birds following farmer tractors often became dizzy and lost a few tail feathers. But this was not as serious as what is happening today.

Smart birds like sparrows do not follow behind tractors. Farming machines belch exhaust fumes. This smoke is dangerous.

Smart birds like black Crows sit patiently on high electric wires, waiting until cars and other machines pass by. They do not suffer from dizziness, blind eyes, or feather loss. We have never seen bald Sparrows. We have never seen bald Black Crows.

"My tests indicate that it is dangerous for birds to fly in sky zones where airplane engines leave their vapors. These vapors are like poison wine. They make many Geese dizzy and drunk. This is why many fly and die.

"We have rules that birds, especially smaller birds, should avoid flight above tree lines. The poison air that airplanes leave is very deadly. Airplanes use deadly fuels that cause hair or feather loss. This is why birds have become naked. This is also why clouds are suffering and become fat from feathers. It is up to us to act smarter. You will not lose feathers if you stay below tree lines. No more high-flying.

"So now you know why Mr. Eagle has a bald head. He flies high, but he does not follow airplanes. This is why he never is dizzy or gets drunk from airplane fumes. He is happy to be alive even if he does not smile."

Hearing these words everyone laughs and clap their hands. The Wise Owl praises Chickee-Lickee-Lee over-and-over again. She feels very special.

Chickee-Lee is honored

Even the Baldy Eagle blinks his eyes rapidly in appreciation for Chickee-Lickee-Lee's report. And Wise Owl turns his head around spinning like a toy top five or six times.

Soon, the clouds become thinner and happier. They are no longer stuffed with feathers. They can drink water without choking.

The future looks brighter. As the days and weeks move on, naked birds grow back their feathers. Many are satisfied to fly below the tall trees. After this problem passes, creatures at Paradise Farms have greater respect and admiration for Chickee-Lickee-Lee.

They sing about her because she is helpful, caring, and responsible. The sun even winks behind a few clouds. Then it begins to rain soft showers. A giant colorful rainbow appears in the sky. The plants and trees sway slightly in the cool evening breezes. Everyone is happy indeed.

Paradise Farm Residents Celebrate Happy Skies

IIII//// THE END /////IIII

AUTHOR

Aaron A. Vessup / aka
"Photoman" creates with
Pen and Cameras.

ARTISTS

Sonny Gergen draws from inspiration, pleasure, and relaxation.

John Salacan is a seasoned devotee to a variety of media forms.

www.ingramcontent.com/pod-product-compliance
Lightning Source LLC
LaVergne TN
LVHW072246060825
818057LV00031B/126
9798892285476